FILL ME IN

The Human Canvas Initiative
Colouring Book

Matti McLean

This project was an accident. A happy amalgamation of fear, passion and opportunity.

It was 2012 and I had just quit my job at a local coffee shop. With no idea what was to happen in the next few months I went to my roommate and asked to paint him as a way to remember him forever. He obliged, but became confused when I asked him to remove his shirt. In the end, we created an image that would change my life (and that you now have the opportunity to fill in!).

I sought to paint my ten closest friends at the time as a way to remember them. I had hoped that no matter what happened or where I would have to go I would always have their images to remind me of the time that we got to spend together. Most obliged and as I posted the image on my Facebook wall for the first time. Immediately the demand was explosive. More friends were asking me to paint them as well. And then more people I didn't know. It was fantastic and in the first year the project experienced explosive growth evolving from an intimate project with friends into The Human Canvas Project.

As time went on, more and more people began to focus on the project. I was fortunate to receive media attention and it became something much bigger than a simple project to connect people with memories. The pictures became a declaration of acceptance to the world. It also burnt me out many times over.

Over the years I am proud of what I've created, but it has also been a huge struggle to keep it going. I always believed that financially, this project deserves to be done by everyone regardless of their earnings. As such, I've decided to start publishing these books in an attempt to raise enough money to allow this project to continue to touch lives around the world.

In short, we are all art. I thank you for your love and support in this initiative and can't wait to see what the future has in store for us!

THE TESTER PAGE
Whether it's markers, crayons or
paint use this page to test them out!
Markers and ink based items are
known to bleed through papers!

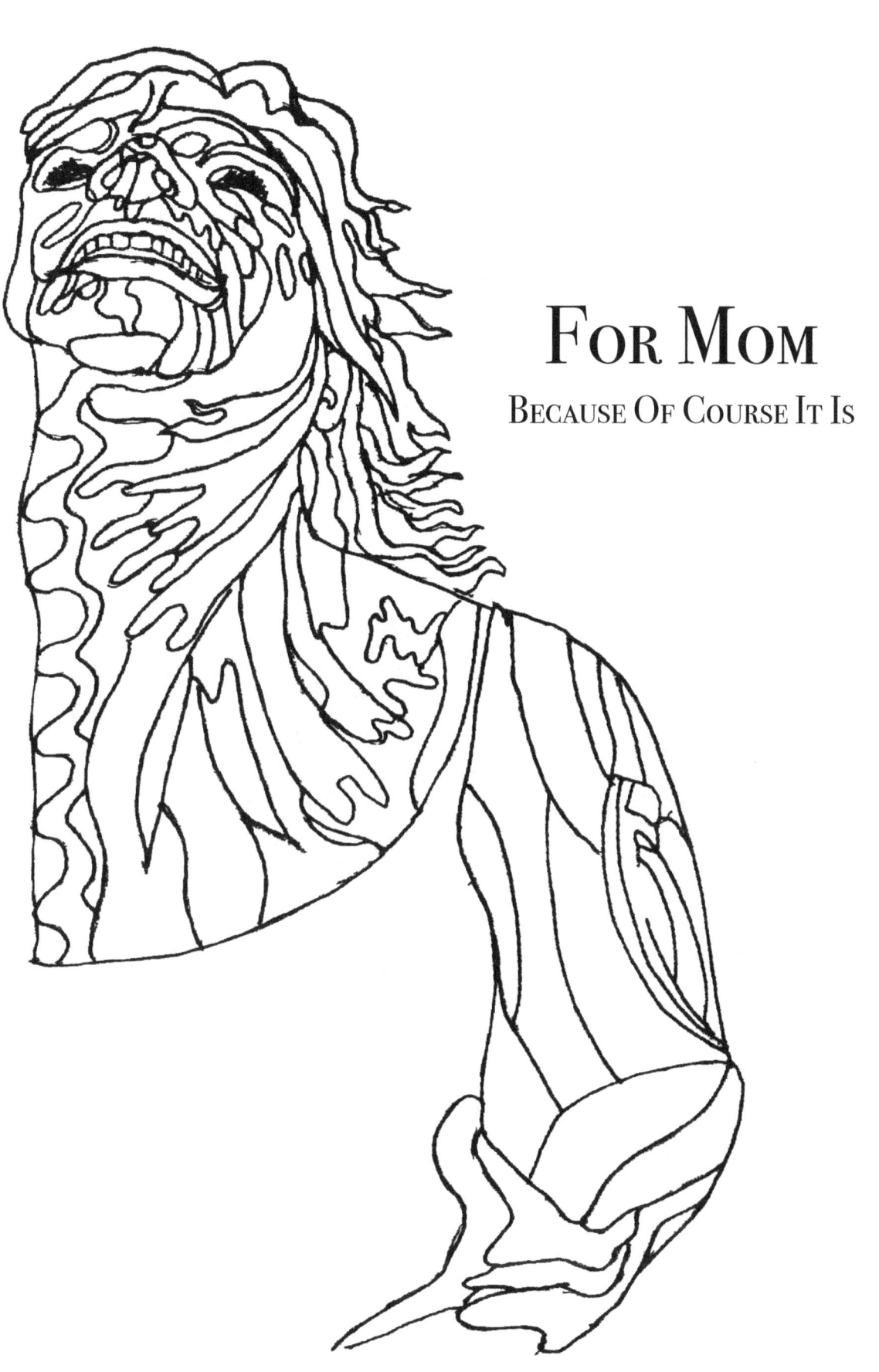

FOR MOM

BECAUSE OF COURSE IT IS

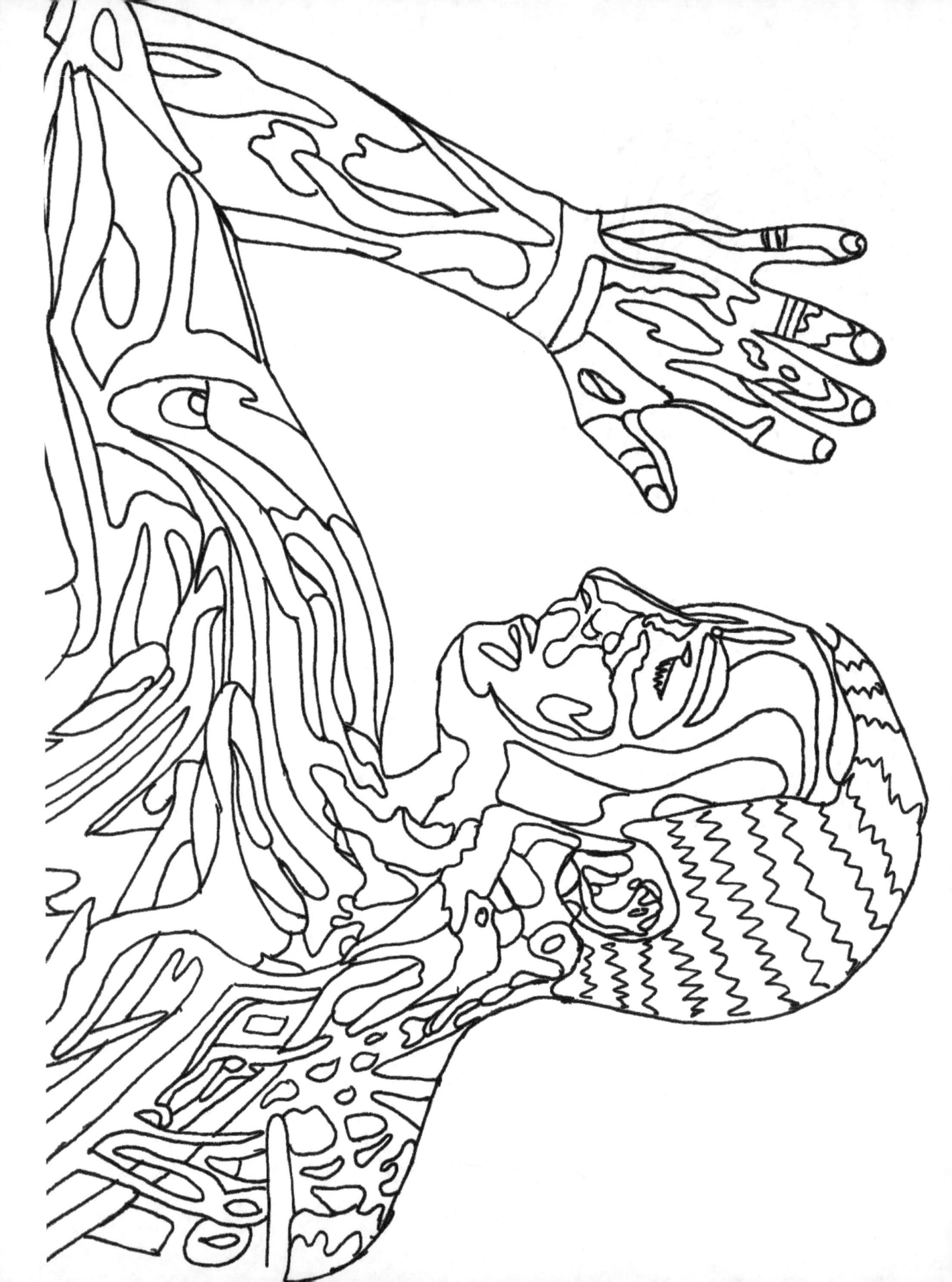

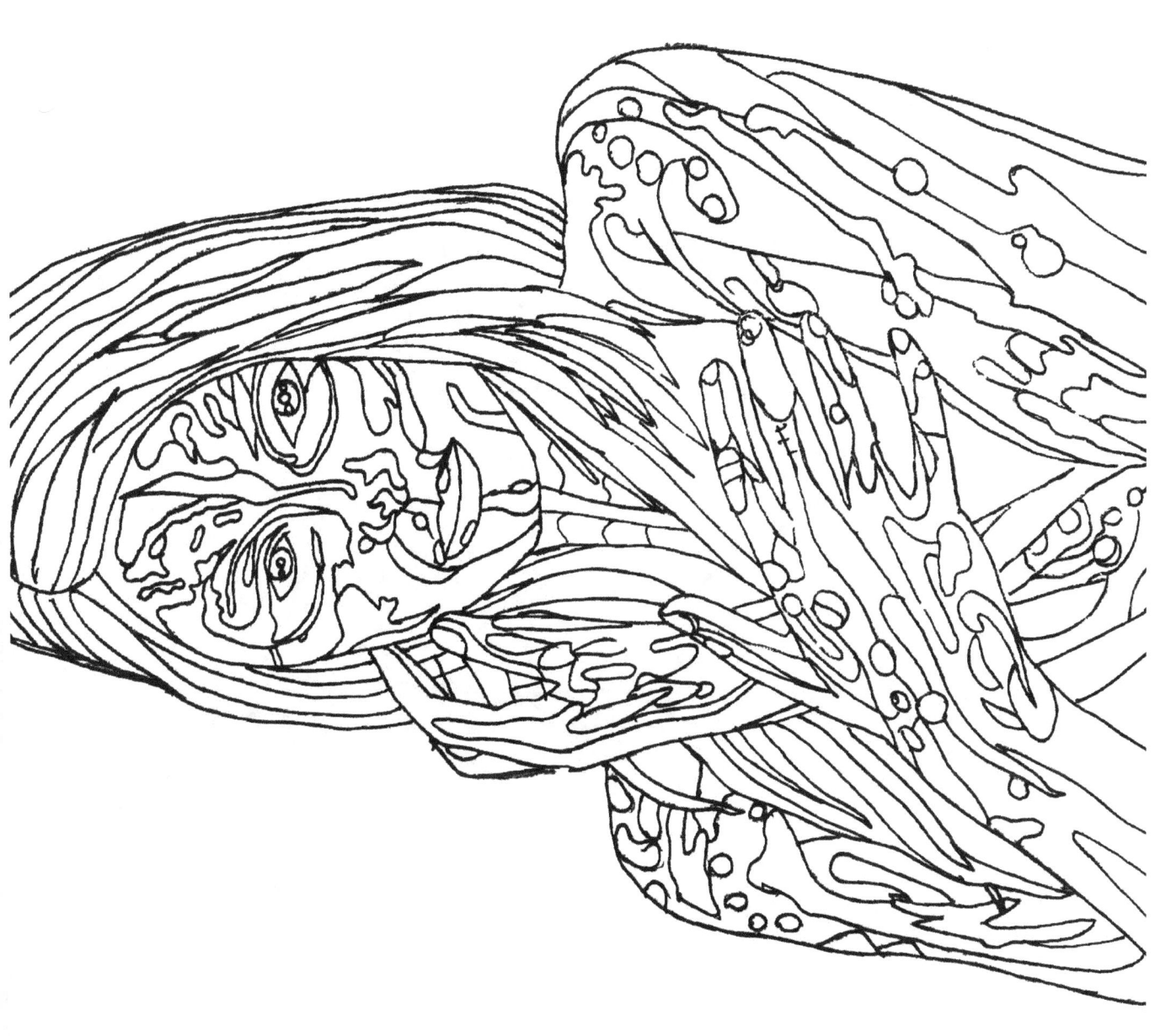

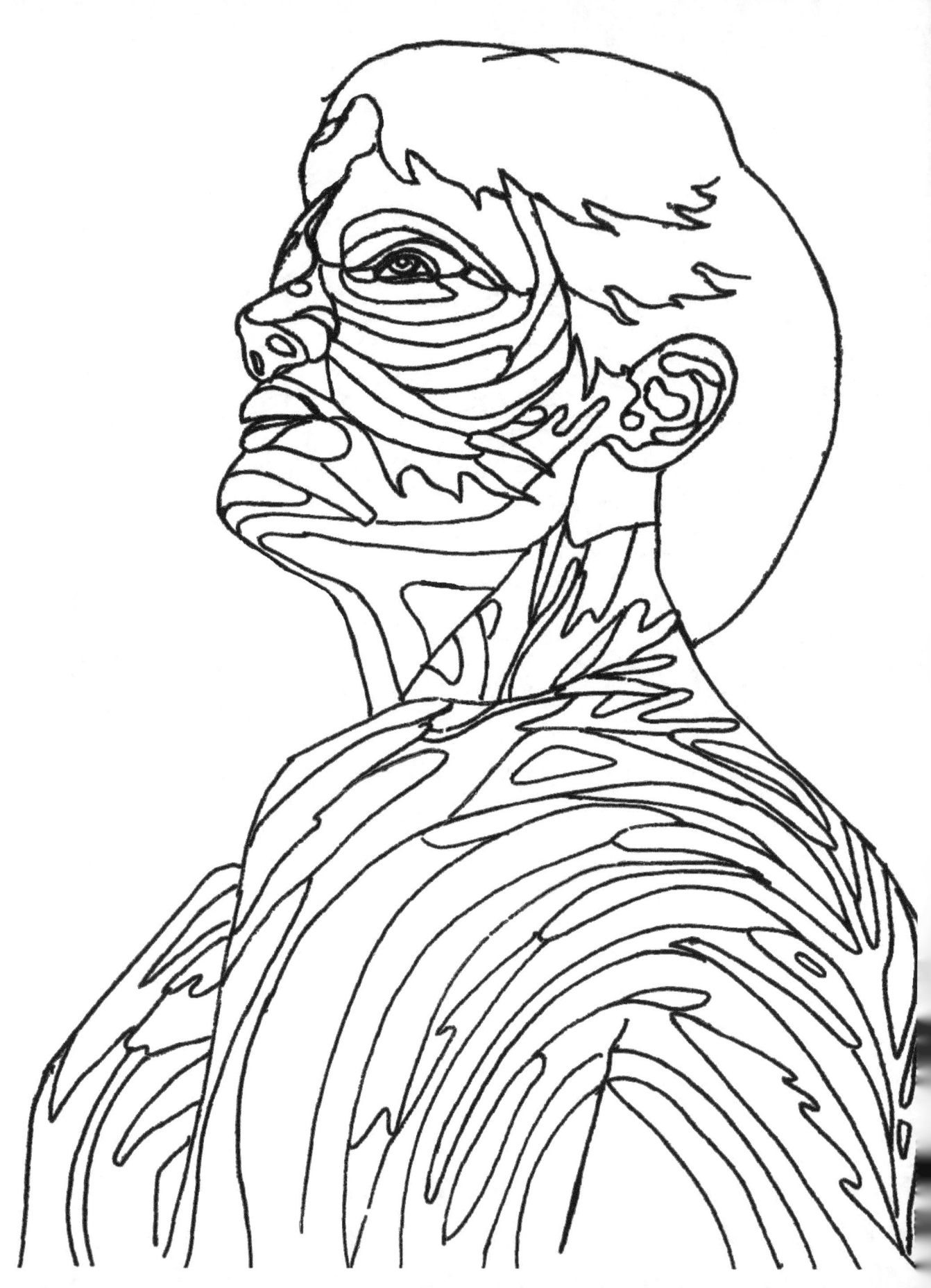

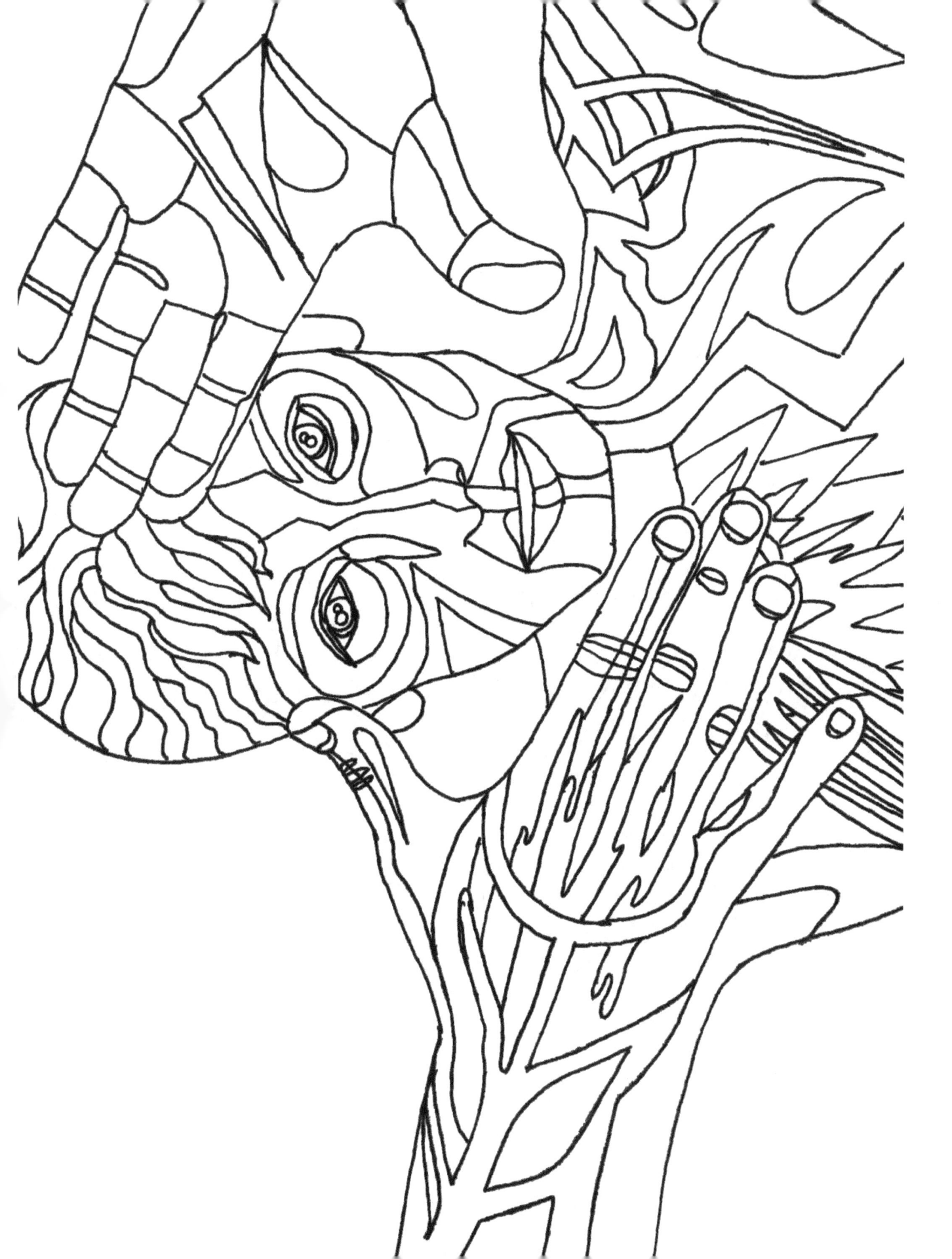

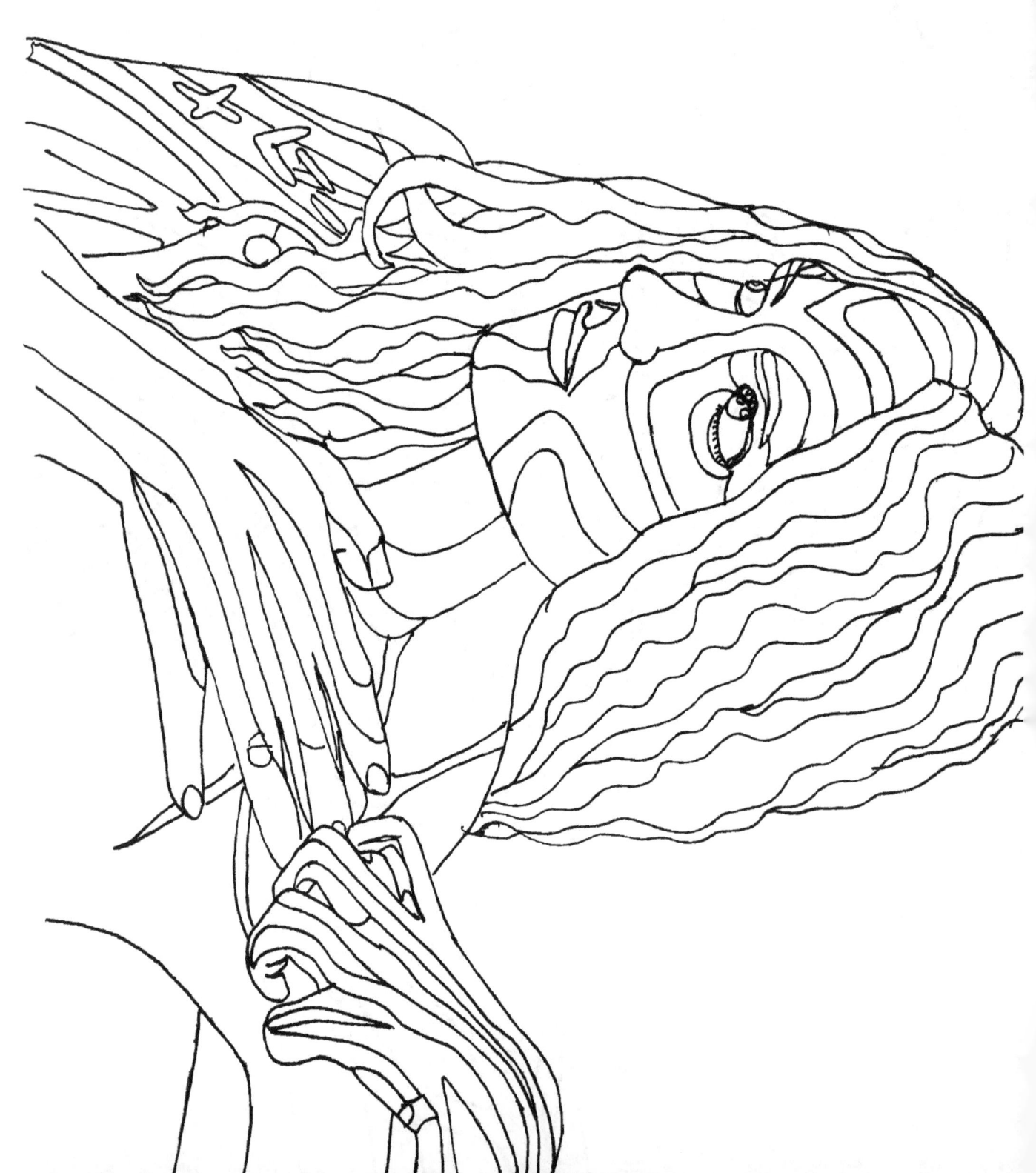

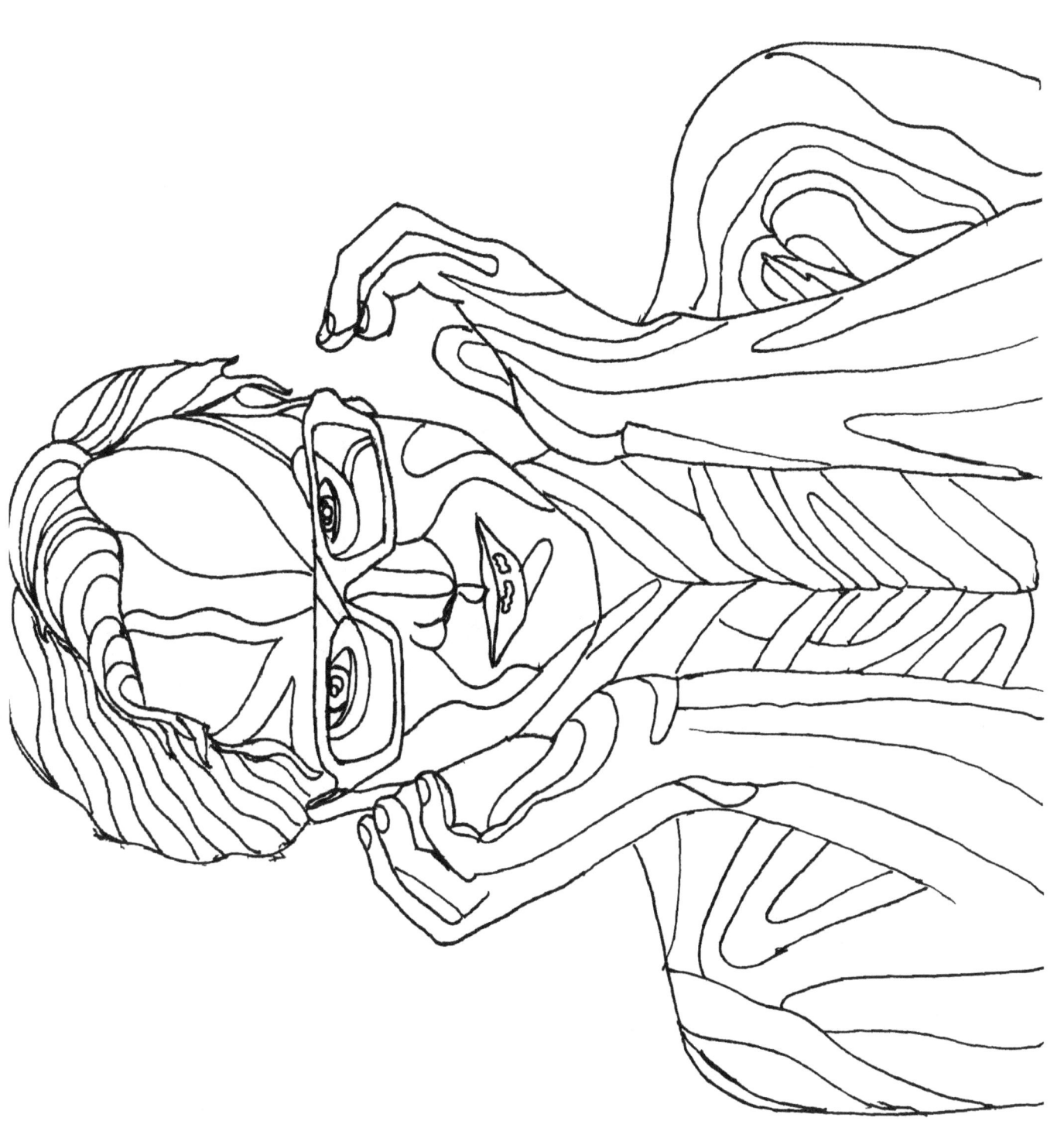

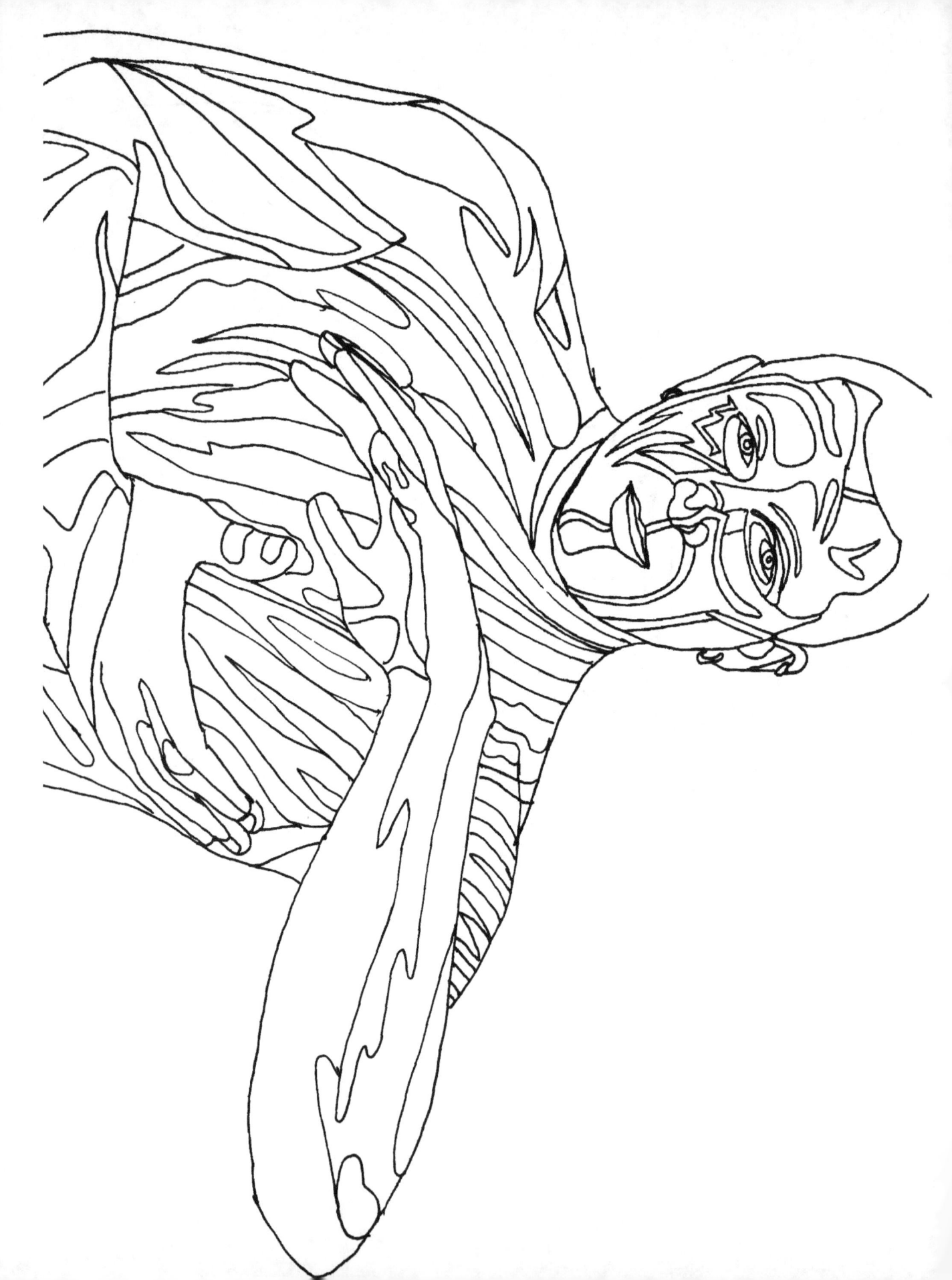

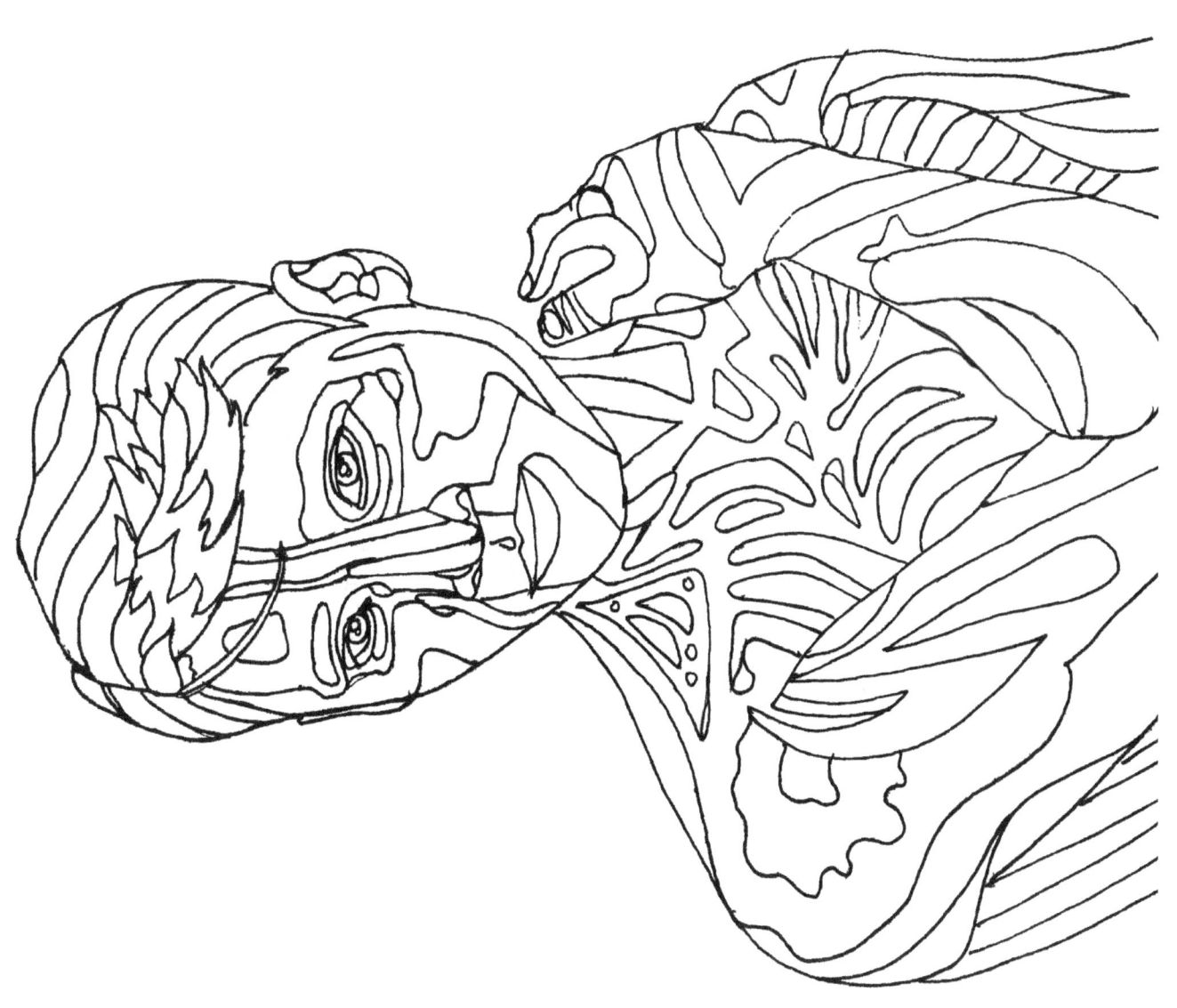

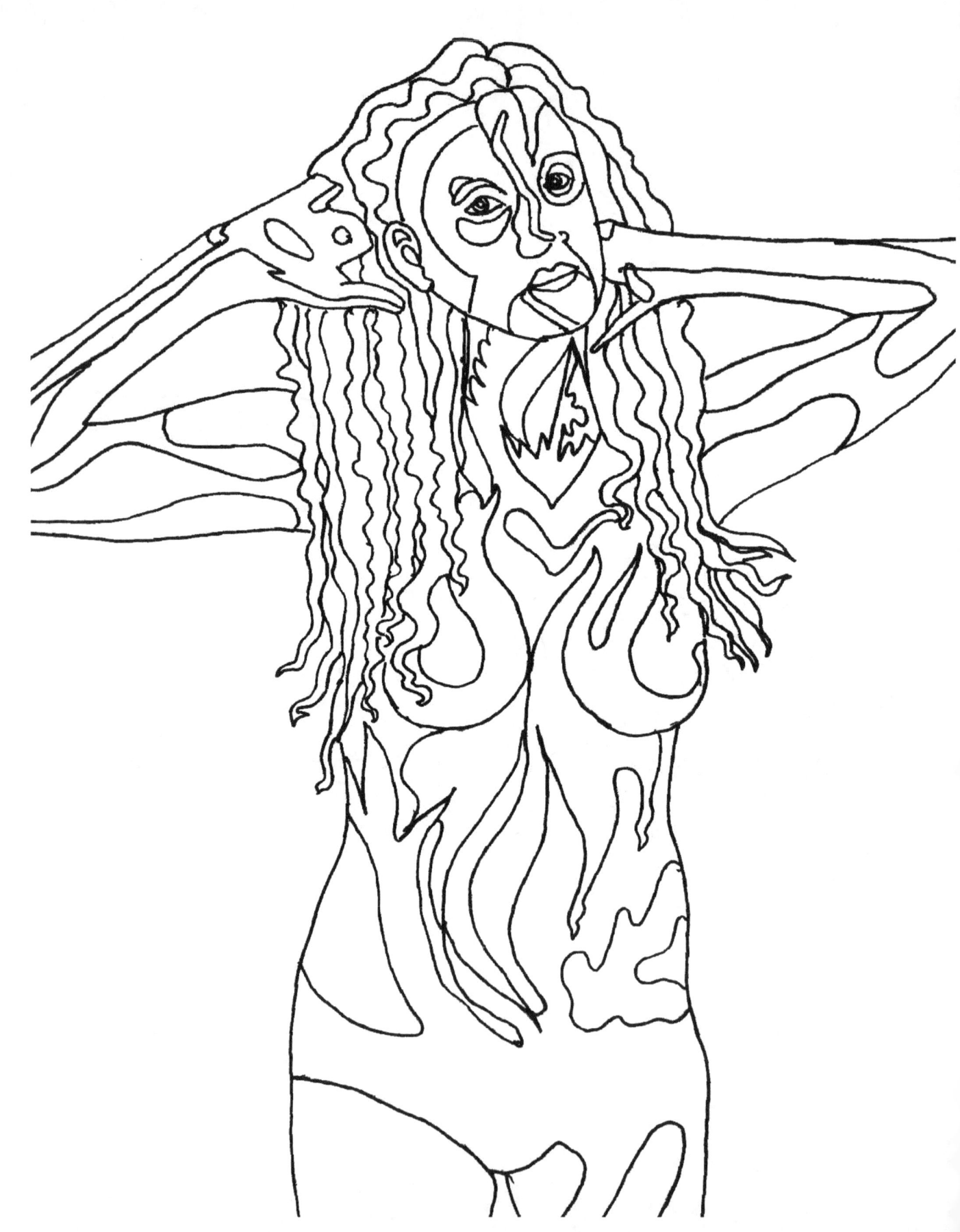

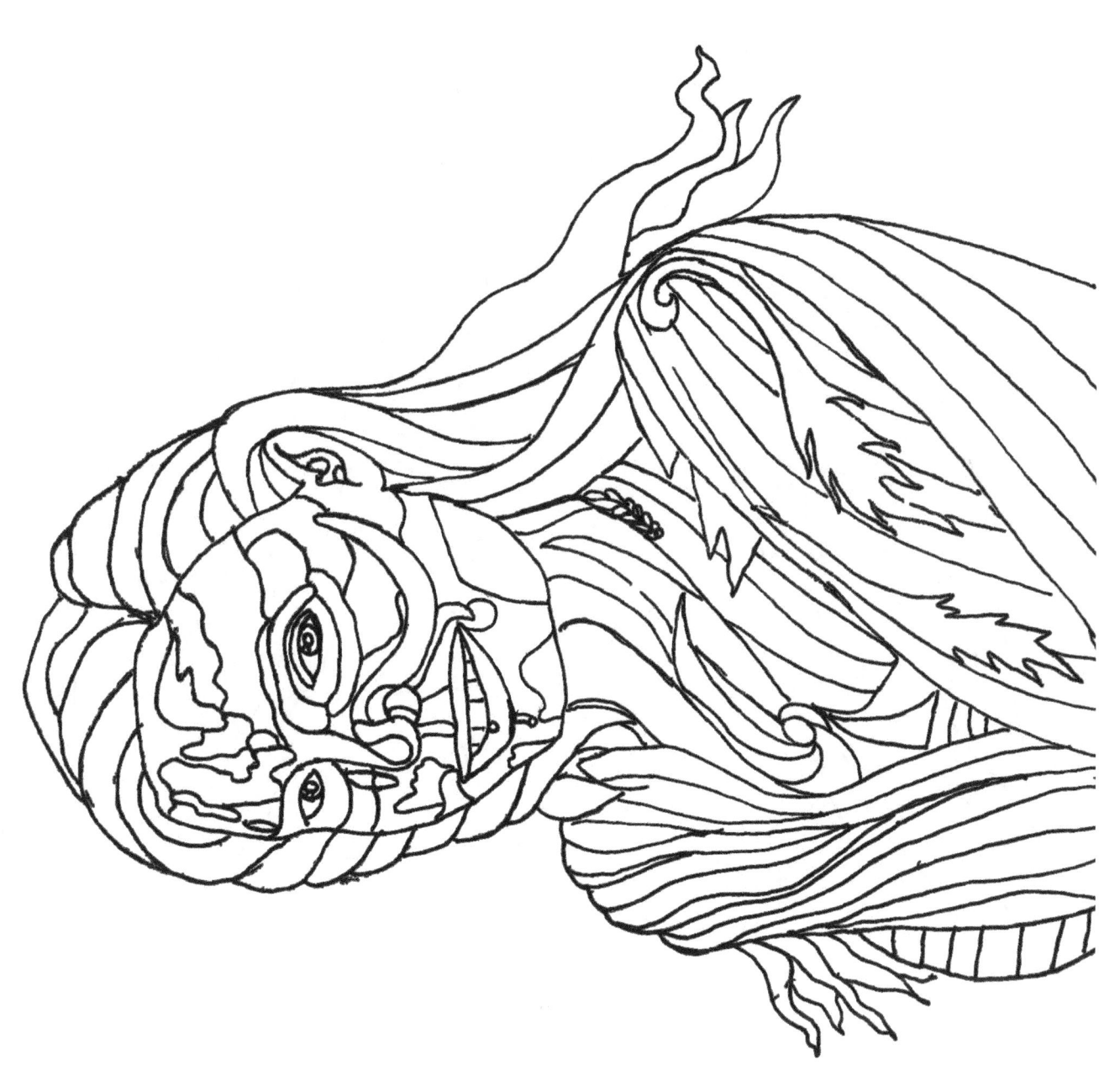

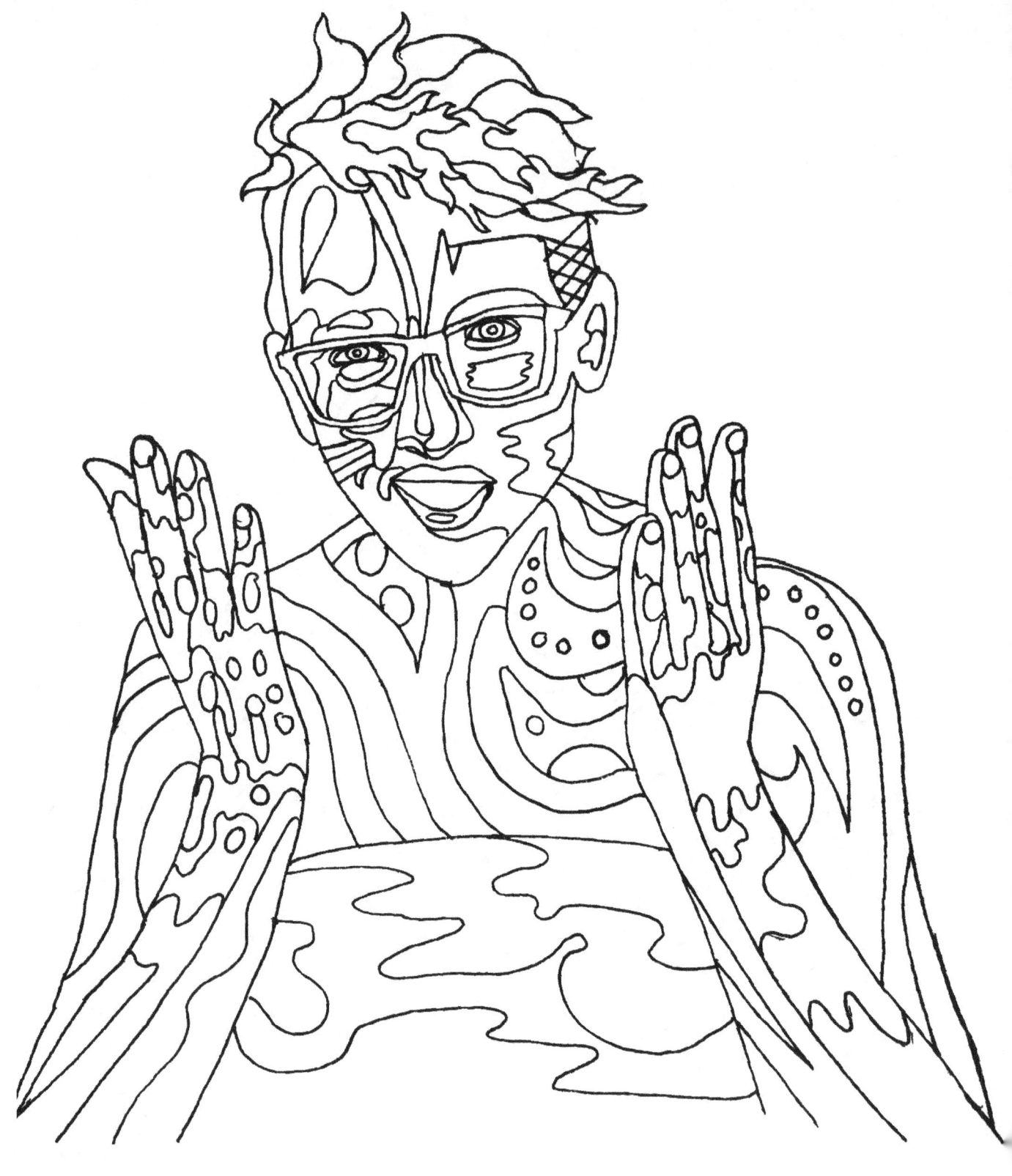

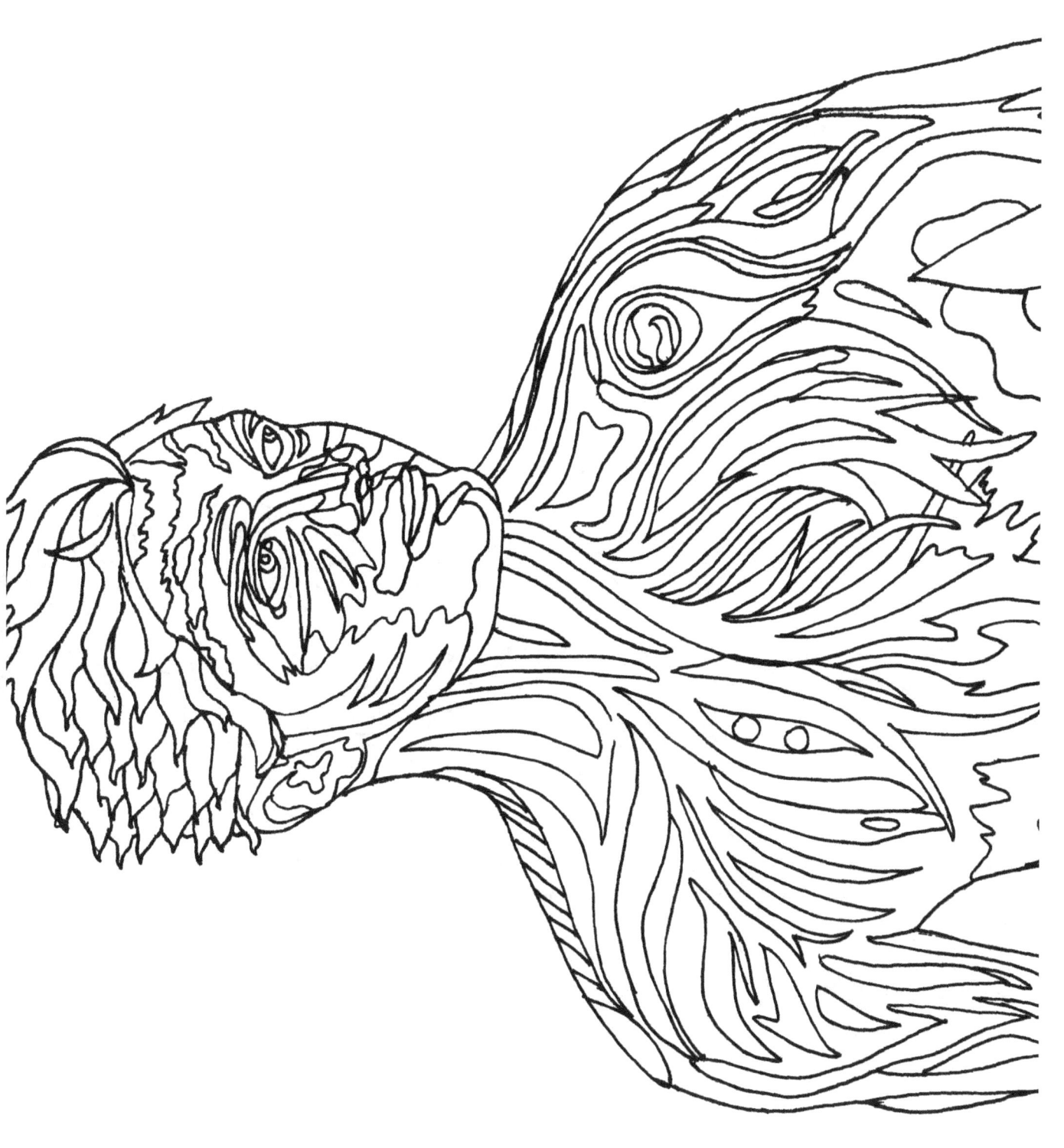

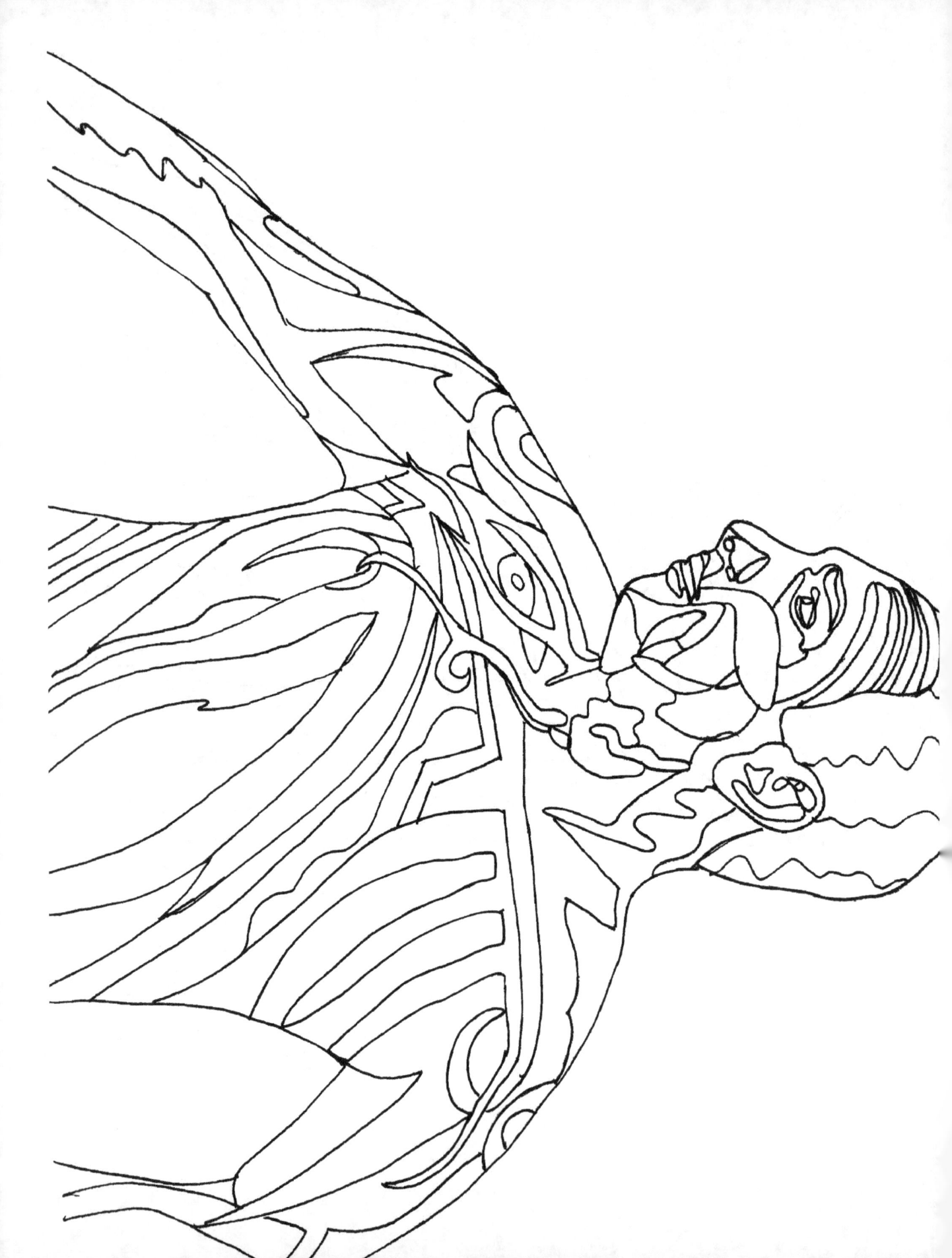

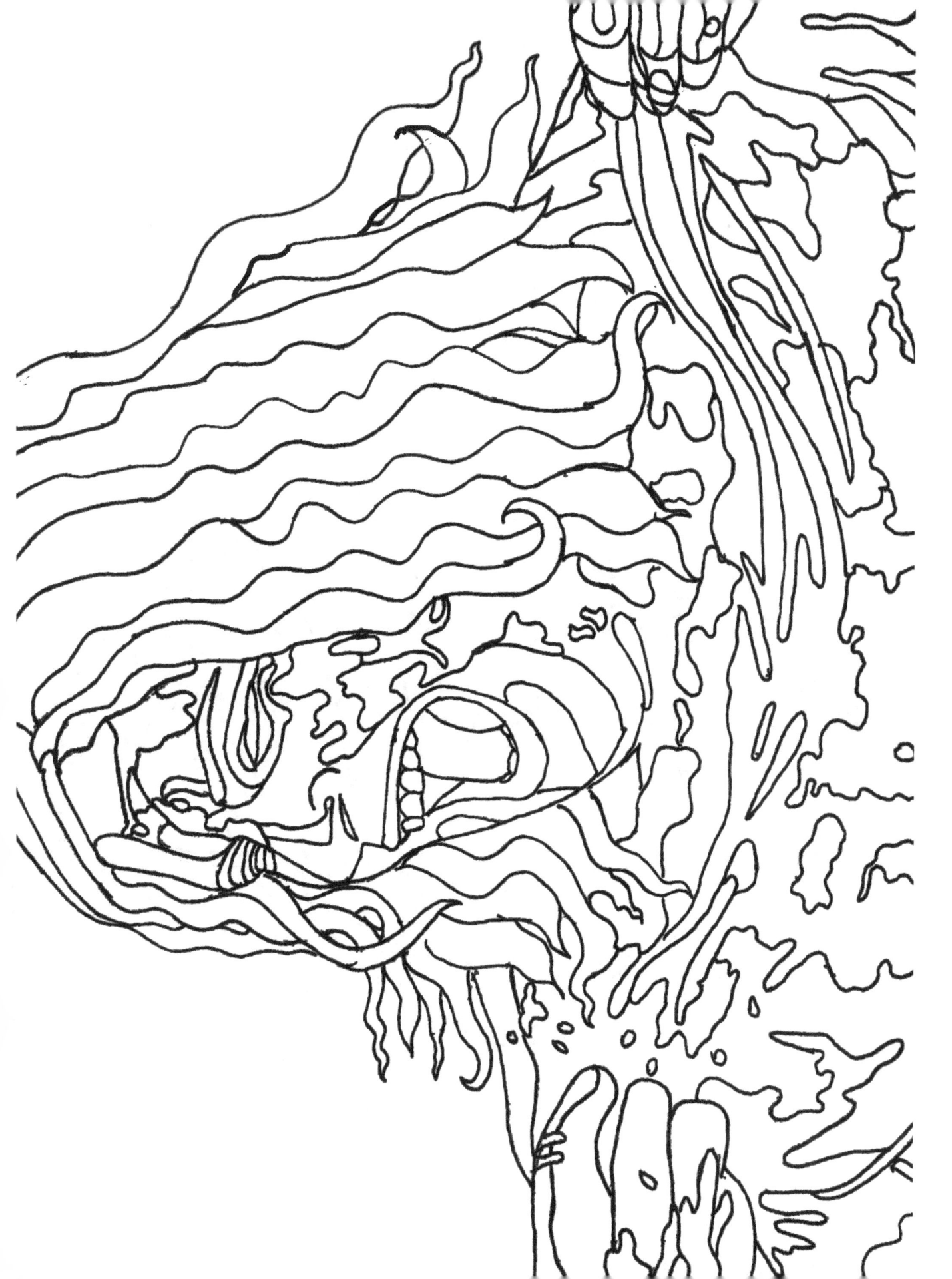

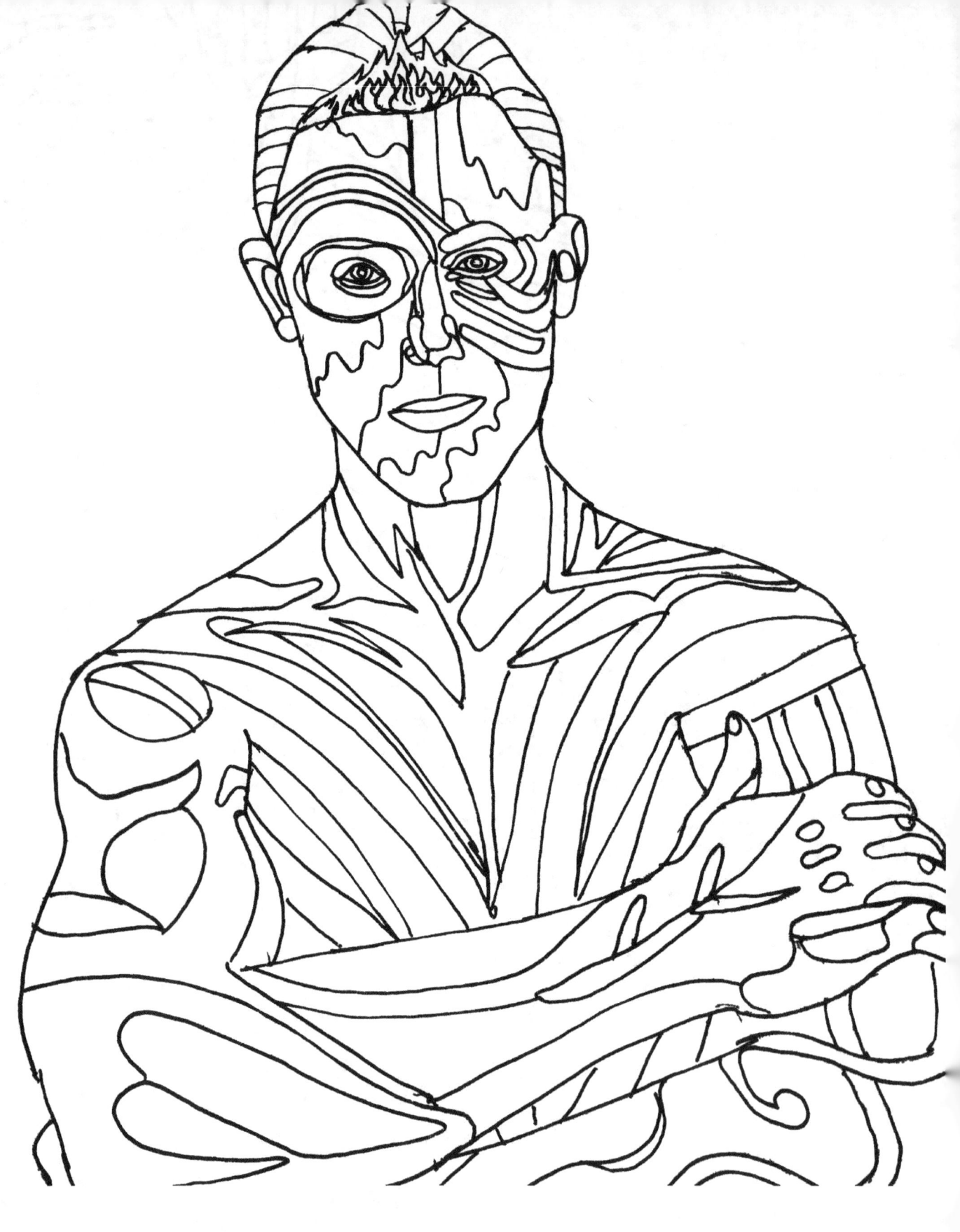

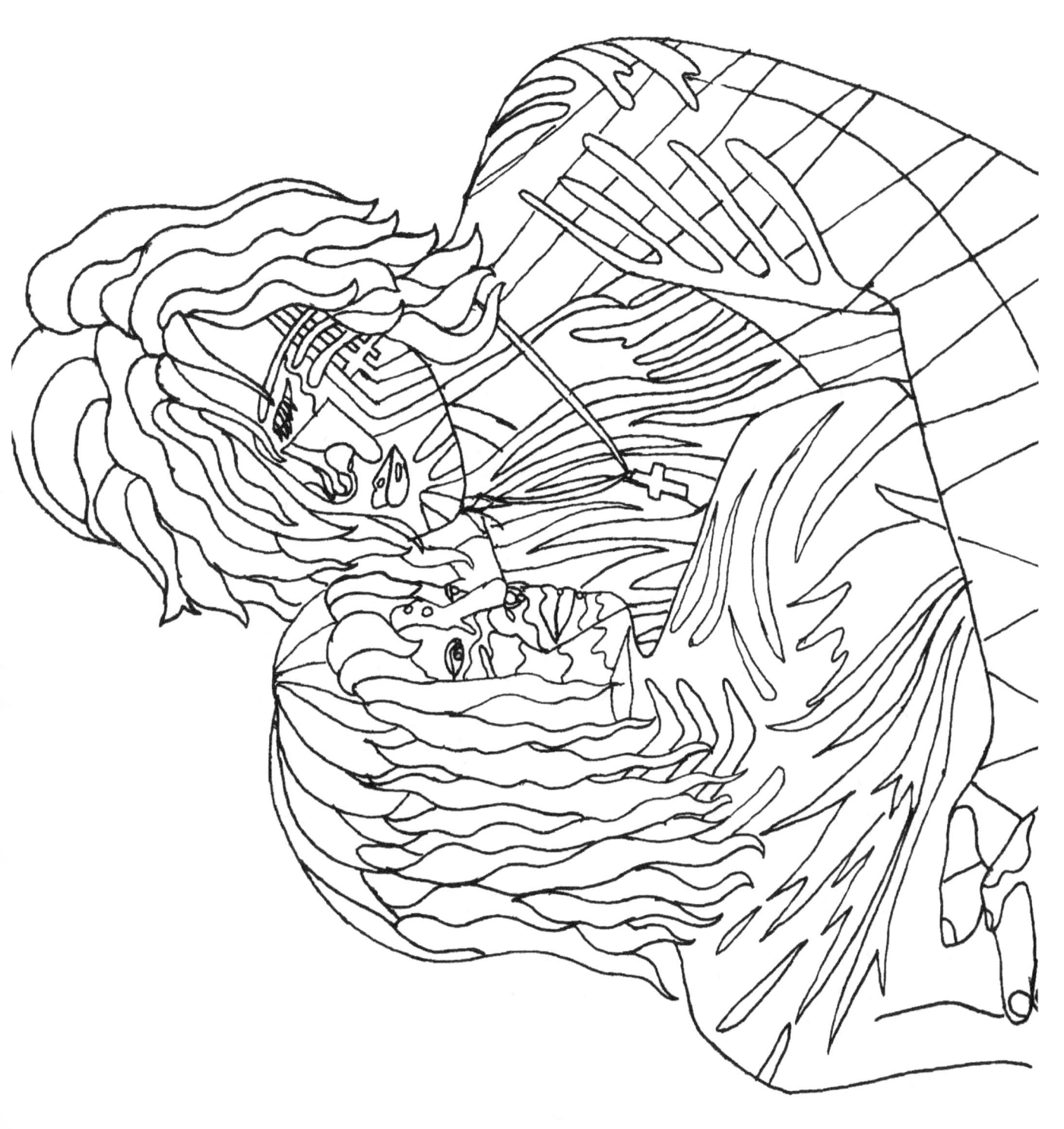

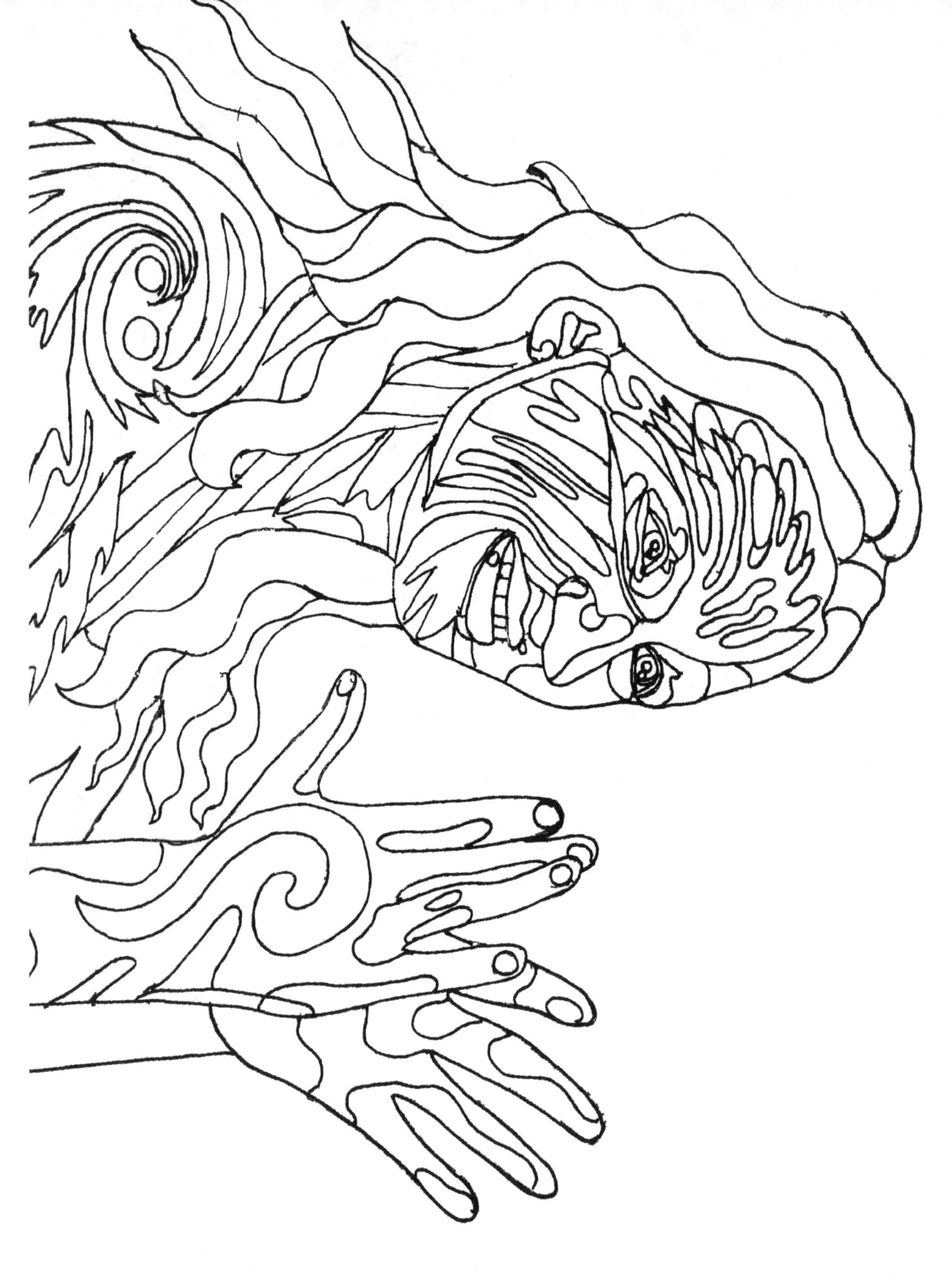

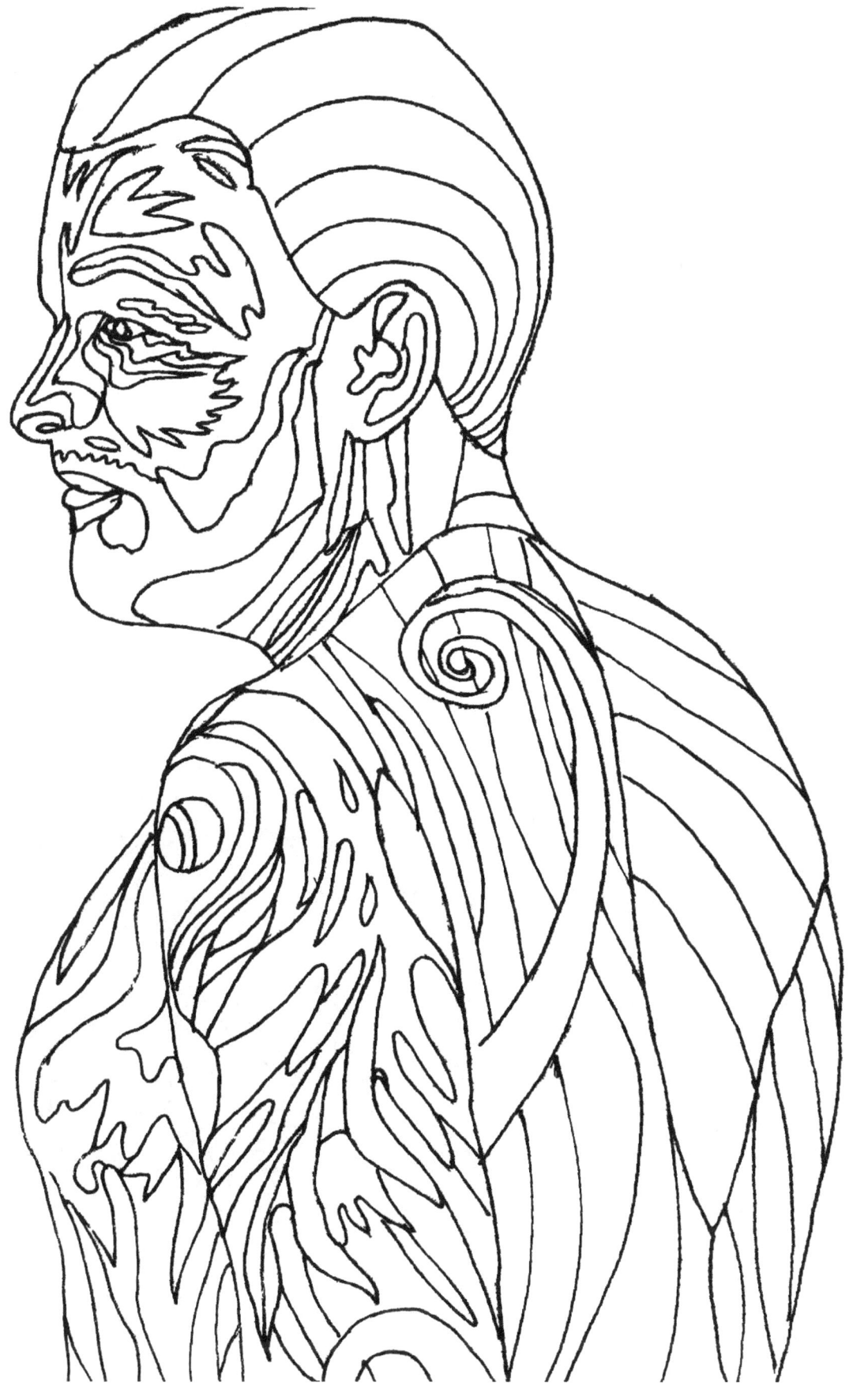

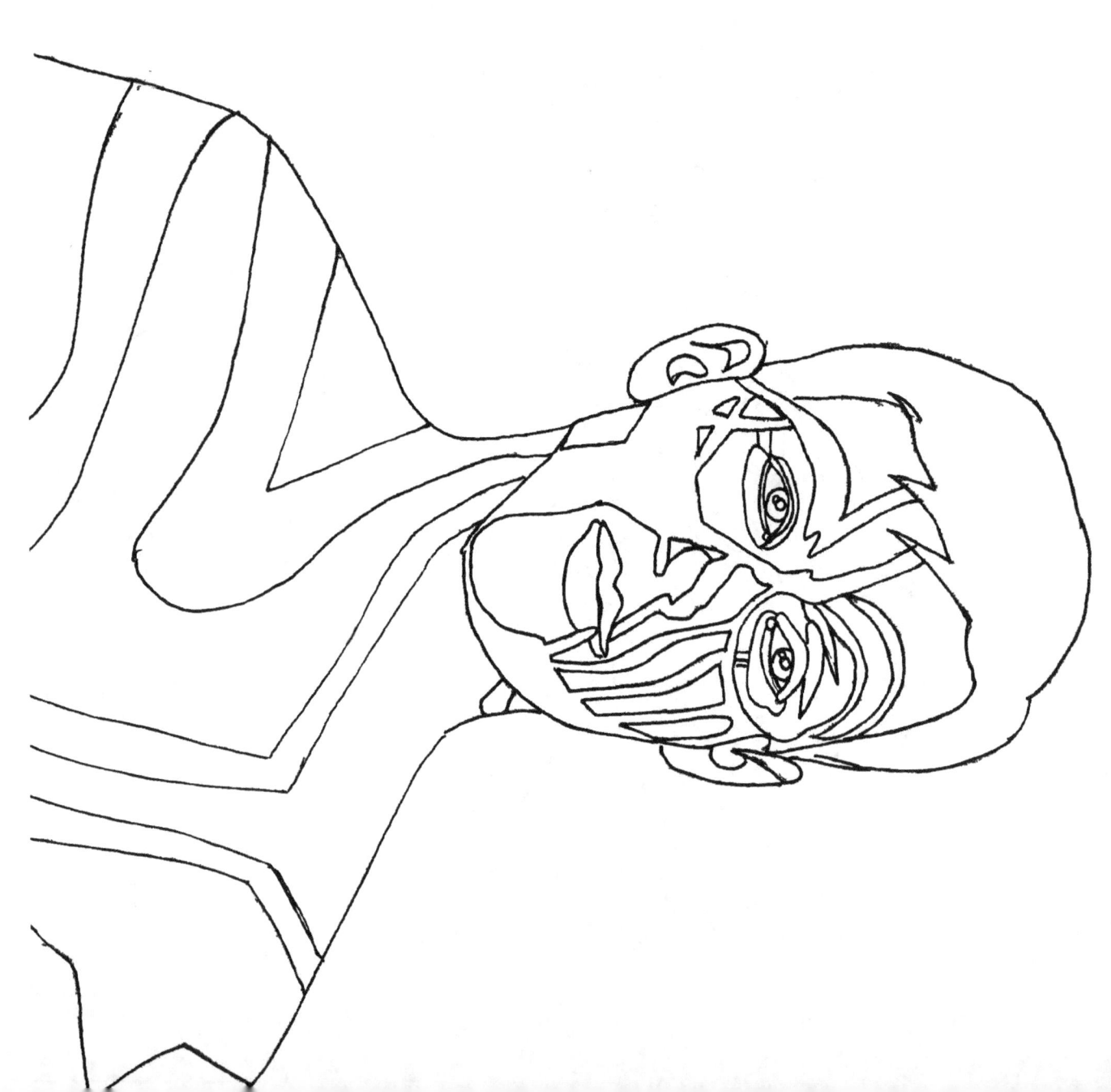

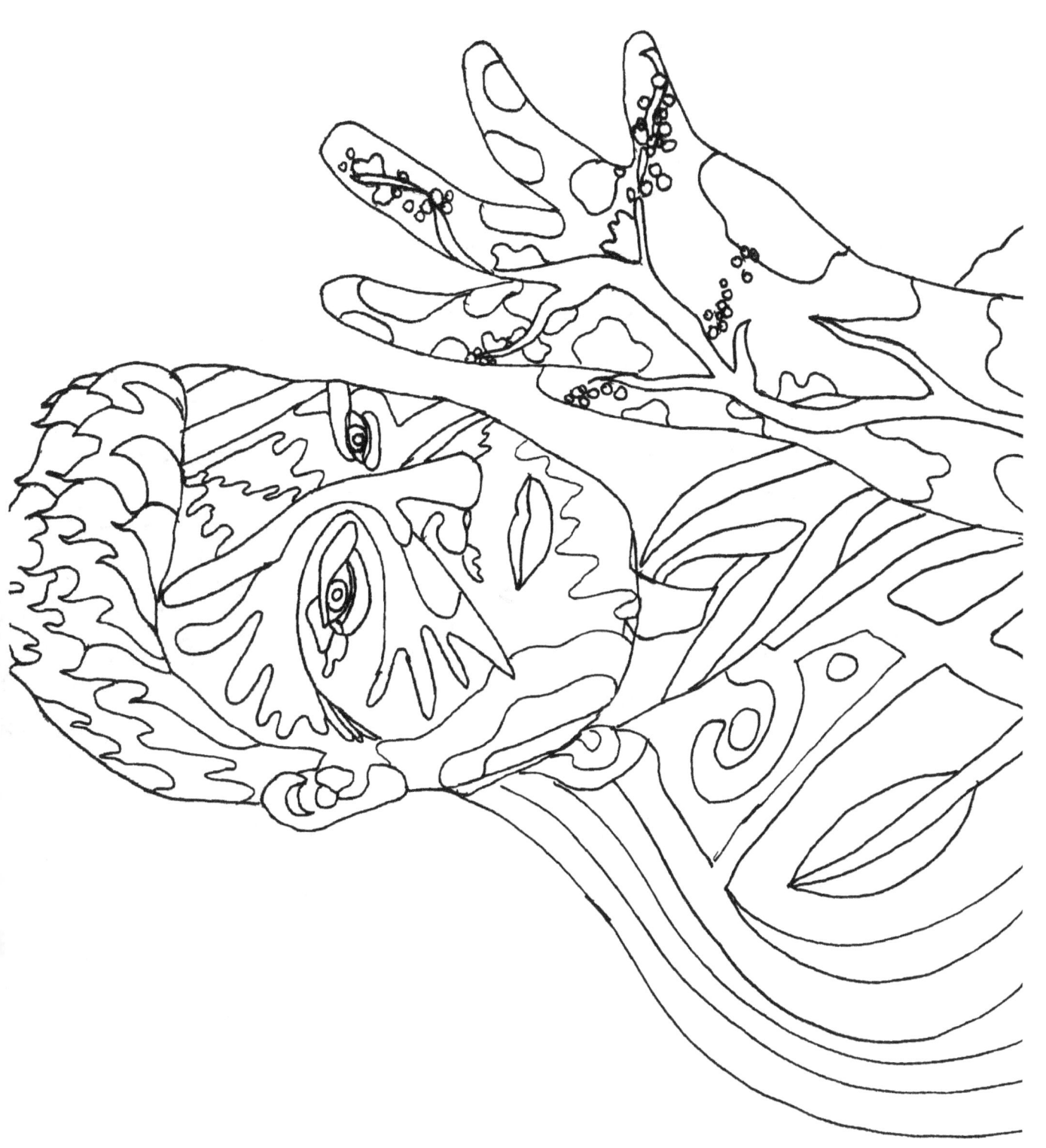

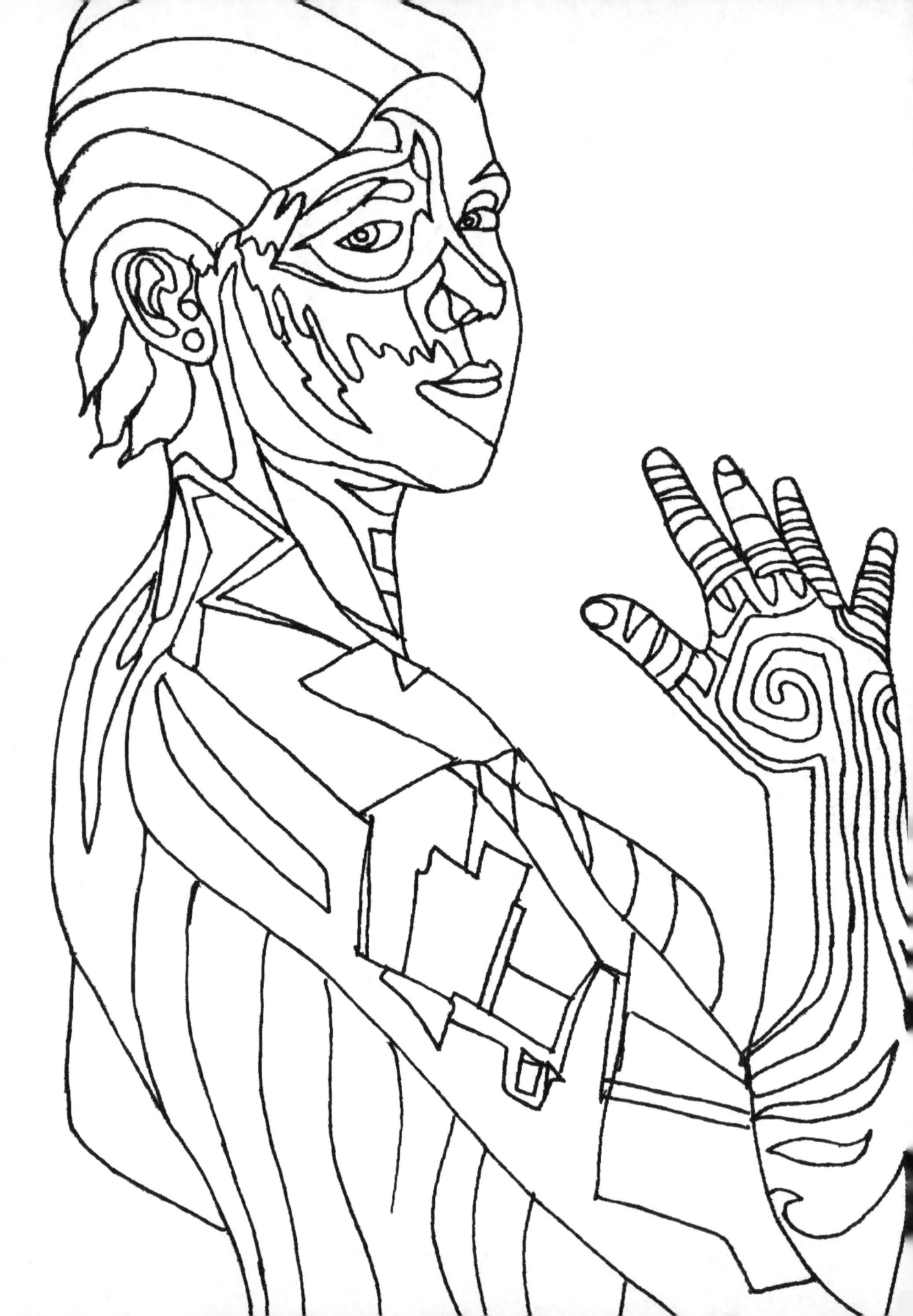

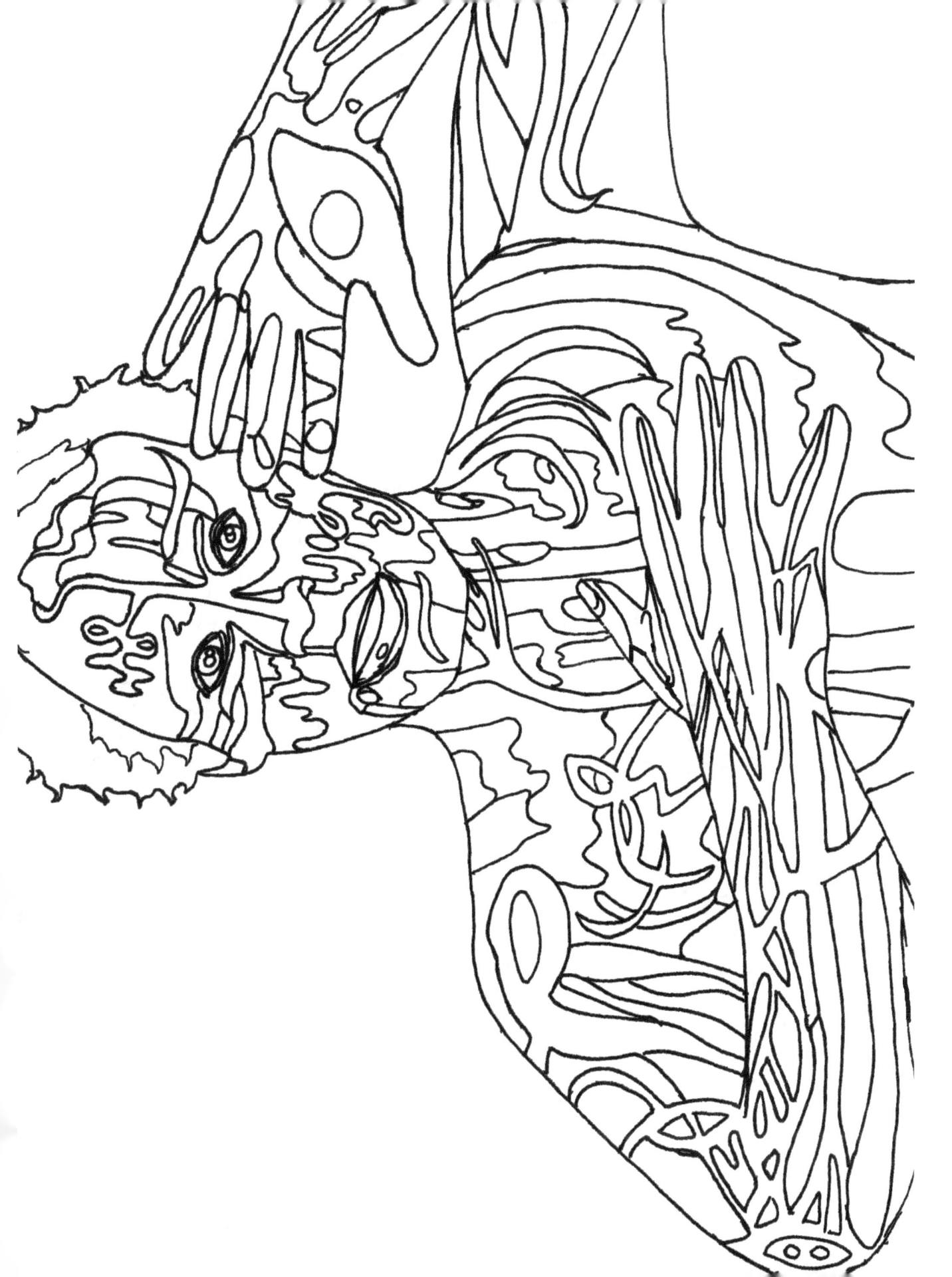

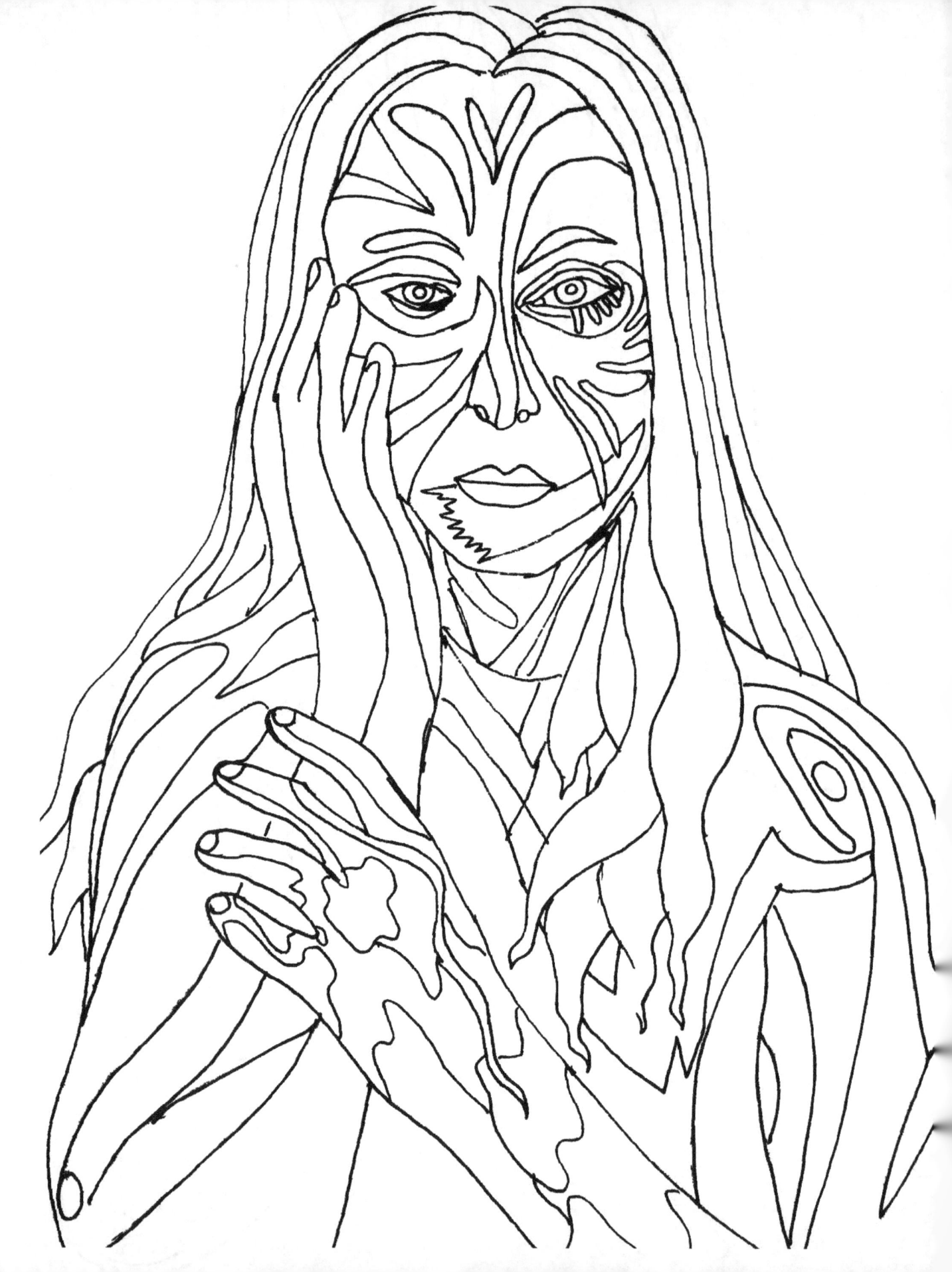

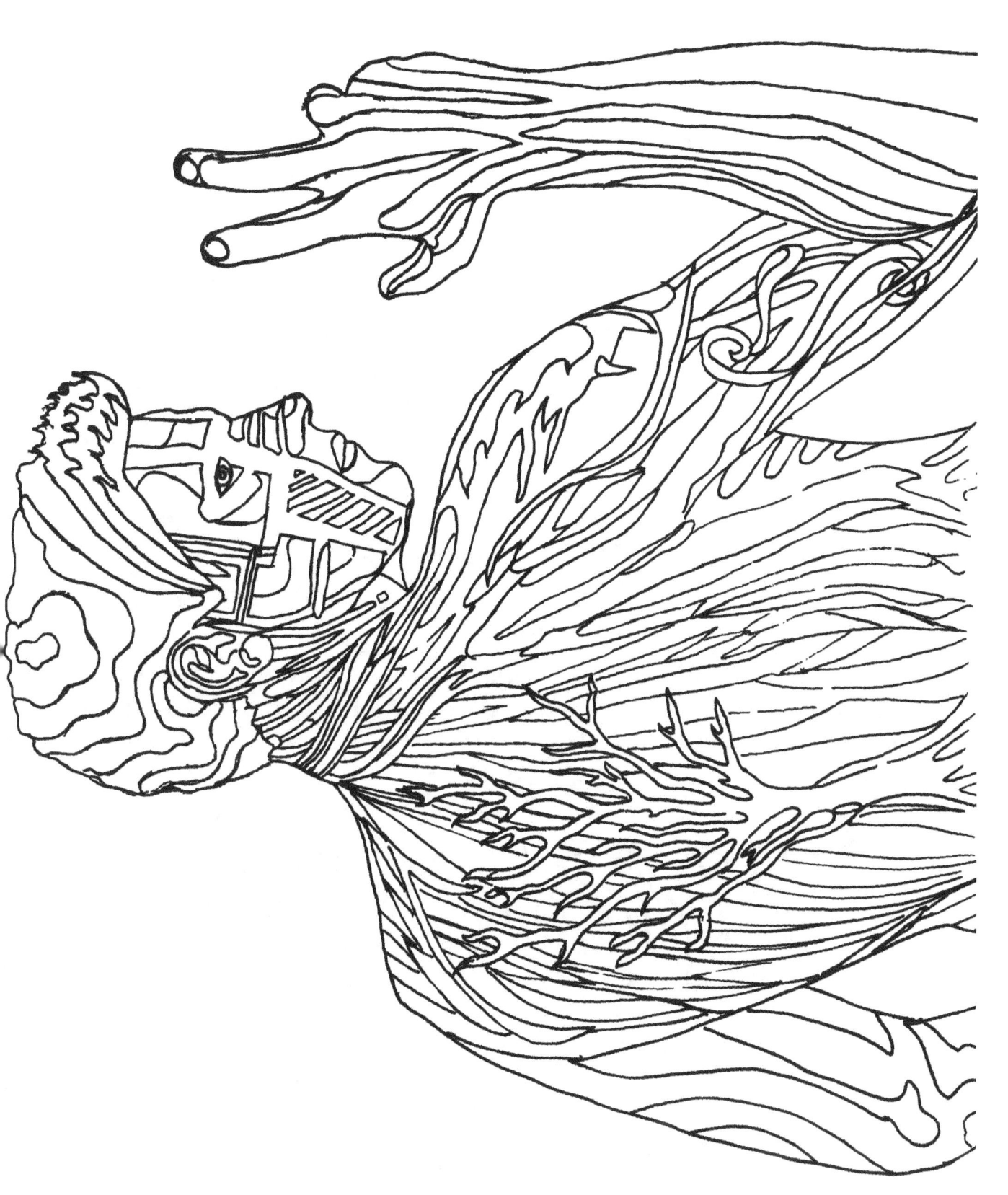

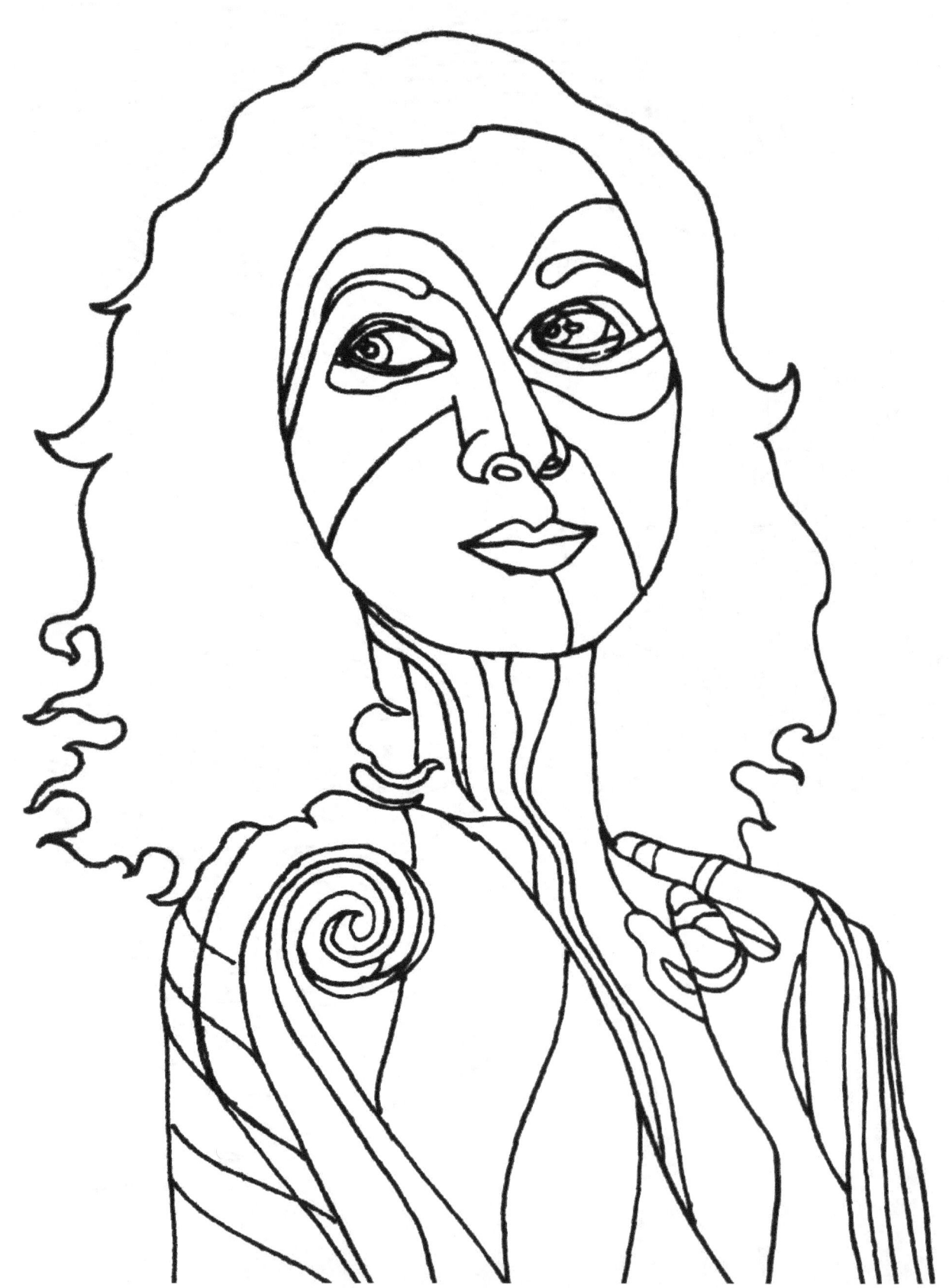

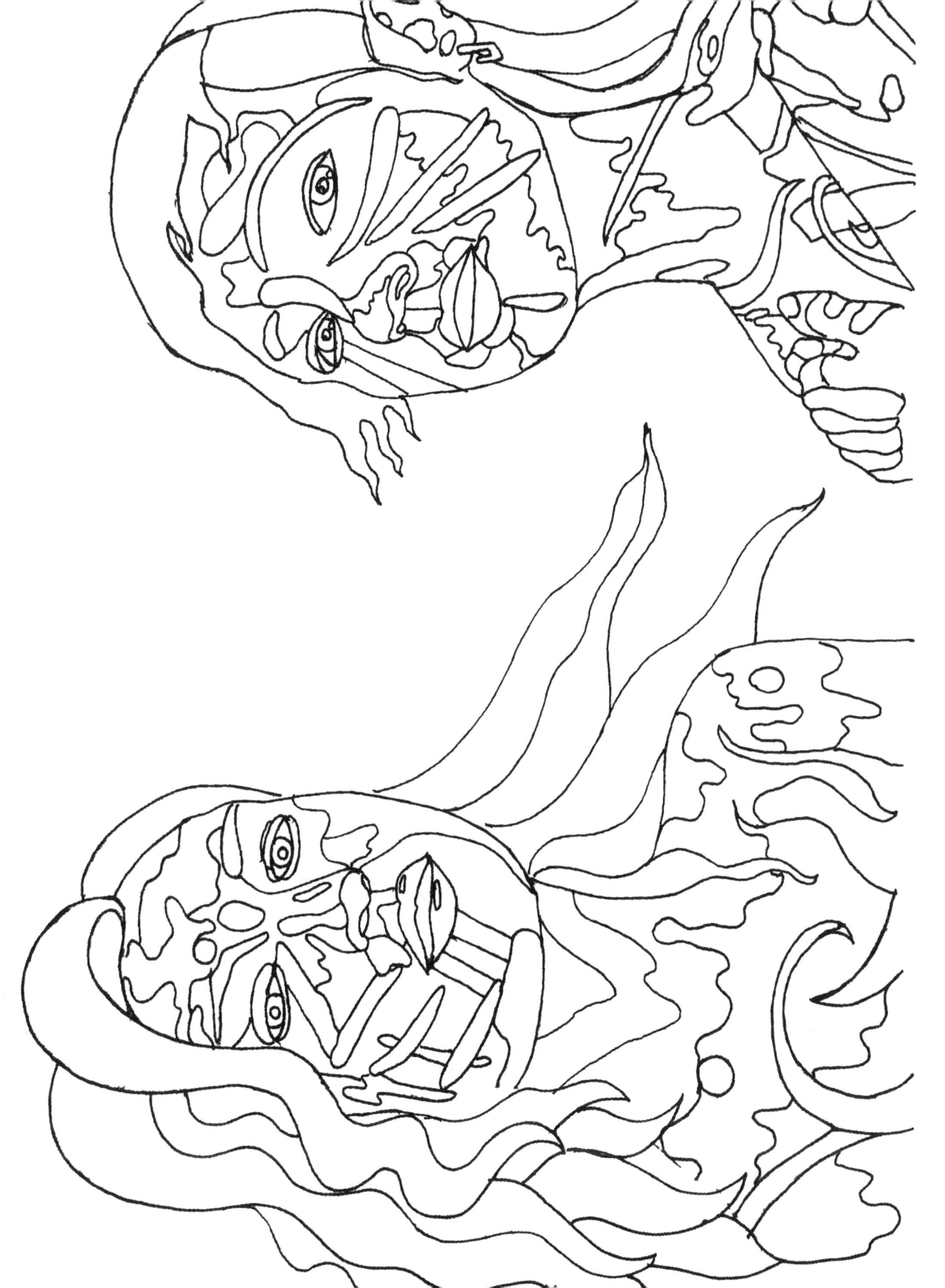

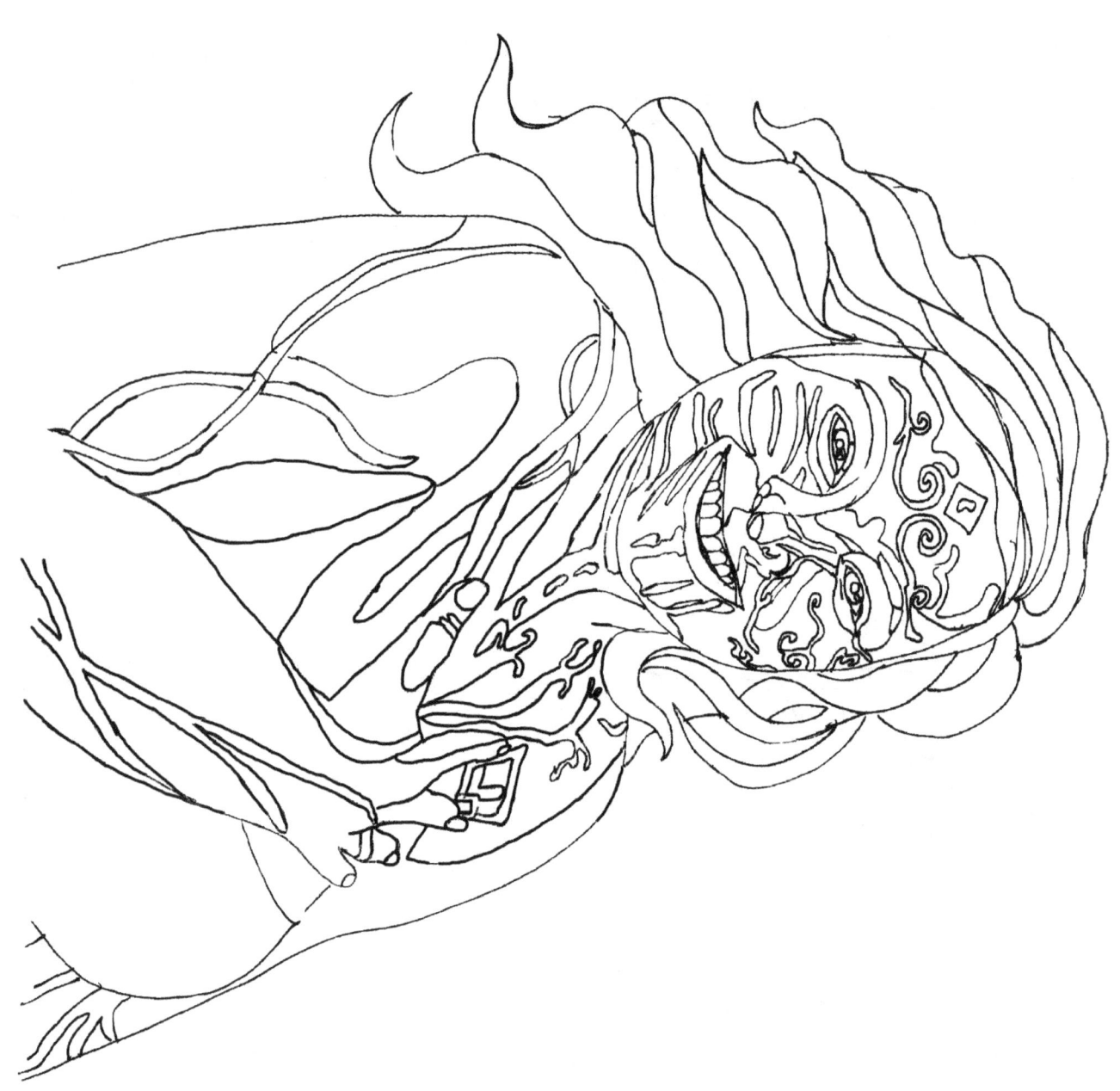

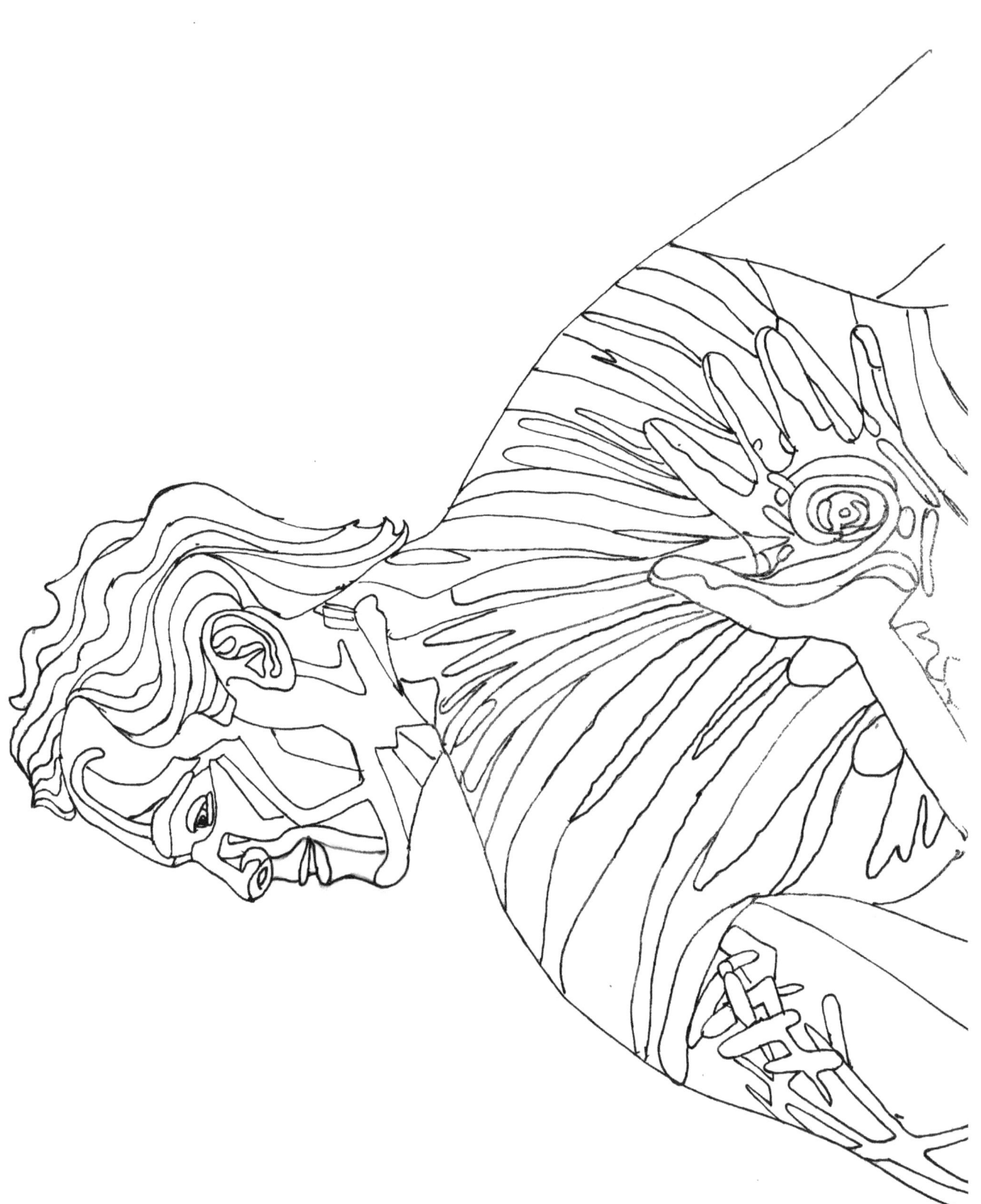

www.ingramcontent.com/pod-product-compliance
Lightning Source LLC
Chambersburg PA
CBHW080529190526
45169CB00008B/3103